CW01551419

Faro & The Algarve Travel Guide

Attractions, Eating, Drinking, Shopping & Places To Stay

Lily Atkins

Table of Contents

Faro

Mainland Portugal's southernmost city, scenic Faro is the capital of the Algarve. A colourful town marked by long sandy beaches and flanked by dramatic rocks. Born inside medieval walls, the city unfolds its long story; one of a mish-mash of influences and periods of both prominence and devastation.

Unfortunately, most foreign sun-seekers are often whisked away to other parts of the region shortly upon arrival to Faro, with the town of 50,000 inhabitants serving as a main gateway to the wider Algarve area. By doing so, they are overlooking the surprising beauty that is Faro – endless sweeping beaches, a historic old town and a delightful National Park all on its doorstep, waiting to be explored.

The scenery in Faro is unlike what one finds elsewhere in Algarve, where steep cliffs, majestic rocks and wild waves dominate the landscape. Here, tranquil waters and white sands are the ruling elements, making Faro a particularly good bet for family beach vacations.

Step away from the sand and you will find yourself wandering around the charming and compact old town. Lose yourself in the pedestrianized meandering streets paved with lovely mosaics and don't forget to take every chance you get to catch breath-taking views towards Faro's harbor. The historic center is endlessly alluring with its period architecture, landmark arches and the magnificent cathedral. What survives here stands as a proud and characterful testament to an oft-painful history, one marked by war tragedies and natural catastrophes.

The lagoon of Ria Formosa has been inhabited since the Paleolithic age. During the Roman occupation period, a settlement by the name of Ossonoba stood on the location of today's Faro and rose to importance due to its port, fishing and salt industry. A Moorish rule in the 8th century made Ossonoba a vital commercial town, with it briefly becoming a princedom capital in the 9th century.

It was around this time that a different name began being used for the town; called Santa Maria during the period, it later became known as Harun, which gave it its current name. The Moors left a profound mark in Faro's history up until their defeat by the Portuguese King Afonso III during the Reconquista in 1249, when the city became Algarve's most prominent one.

Sacked by the Earl of Essex in 1596 and reduced to shambles, it became secondary to Lagos which had already imposed itself as a capital. This lasted until the historic 1755 earthquake that heavily damaged most coastal towns with the exception of Faro. Although impacted as well, the town was protected by the sandy coast of the Ria Formosa lagoon and its superior sheltered position has lent it the administrative powers it still enjoys today.

Although chances are you will be tantalized enough by Faro to be content to stay here for the full course of your vacation, nearby attractions are sure to beckon you with their proximity and significance. Due to its location in the center of Algarve, Faro is a great base for those wanting to explore the wider region. Tour the magnificent beaches sprinkled around the Ria Formosa Nature Park, explore the ruins in close by Estoi and don't miss a chance to see the yachting lifestyle in the exclusive Vilamoura marina. Whatever you are looking for from your holiday, Faro is sure to deliver.

Culture

The last town on the Iberian Peninsula to be liberated from Islamic rule, Faro's culture is invariably influenced by the diversity of peoples that have inhabited the area during its long history. A notable Moorish stamp is evident in landmarks and the general architecture of white-washed houses, with a certain feeling of an old world culture hard to brush off as you wander the maze of alleys in the center.

To begin to understand some of the history that sets the backbone to Faro's culture, pay attention to the ceramic tiles (*azulejos*) around the old town, which depict historic scenes and provide insight into the complexities of the town's past. Here, Baroque, Gothic and Renaissance styles converge into an architectural fusion, mirrored by the history of the city's most important landmarks; Faro's Cathedral, for example, has previously served as a Roman forum and subsequently a mosque.

For an in-depth coverage of the region's cultural heritage, check out the Municipal Museum chock-full of local ancient artifacts. Nearby Estoi with its Milreu Ruins is a magnet for history buffs where you can find one of the world's oldest churches. Additionally, whiffs of ancient Roman civilizations await you in the Cerro da Vila ruins in nearby Vilamoura.

If you are planning to travel to Faro during August, your visit may coincide with the annual FolkFaro festival (www.folkfaro.com) which takes place August 17-25. The festival is a colorful celebration of the region's folklore, but is also decidedly international, with performers, parades and various shows with worldwide participants.

Location & Orientation

The reason why Faro is a popular entry point for Algarve visitors is the proximity of the airport. At only 5 kilometers away from the city, Faro's airport (FAO) has witnessed a consistent increase of number of travelers, with low-cost airlines flocking to it in recent years.

Connected to the city center by bus and taxi, the airport is a mere 20-minute ride away (€2.20 by bus or about €10 by taxi)

Other options for arrival into Faro include a high-speed train from Lisbon (a 2.5 hour ride) as well as regional trains which connect it to other points along the Algarve coast.

Those wanting to discover the wider region should consider visiting with a vehicle (or hiring one), which will also enable you to explore at will. That being said, bus lines between Faro and a number of other cities on the Iberian Peninsula (including Lisbon, Porto, Madrid and Seville) run daily.

While walking within Faro is an enjoyable way to see the city, consider packing adequate footwear to avoid uncomfortable strolls around the cobblestone streets. If you are planning to use the public transportation within Faro, you should be looking out for buses number 14 and 16, which circulate around the city and travel as far as the airport and the Faro beach. Tickets can be bought on board and cost €2.20.

Climate & When to Visit

A moderate Mediterranean climate, plenty of sunshine and a perpetual breeze make Faro a favorite destination year-round, with the Algarve winter being far from the gray and gloomy scenery found in European vacation spots further north.

Sunny days and temperatures averaging between 12 (54 °F) and 16 C (61 °F) are the norm here during winter, though you should be prepared for frequent rain if you choose to visit Faro in the off-season.

Considered one of Europe's sunniest places, Faro's temperatures are pleasant throughout the year. But perhaps the best time to visit it is at very earliest of summer, when the air is still fresh but the sea is comfortably warm for a swim. Be prepared for a few colder nights up until June, and pack a change of warmer clothes just to be sure.

A lot of visitors prefer the months of July and August which can be considerably warmer and significantly busier. Average daily temperatures range between 27 and 35 °C (81–95 °F). But regardless of how hot it gets, the pleasant sea breezes are sure to help you keep your cool. The warm weather stretches well into fall, with October temperatures sometimes even approaching 30 C (85 °F).

Money & Currency

The official currency in Portugal is the Euro. Prices encountered during your Faro holiday will vary depending on your choice of accommodation, entertainment and itinerary plans. However, as Faro is a working city and is often overlooked by tourists, prices here are generally more affordable than in other resorts around the Algarve. In fact, it has been voted as one of the most affordable European beach destinations, with fantastic value accommodation and eating options.

Maps

For an excellent and comprehensive map of Faro city centre, see:
http://www.farouncovered.com/Portals/Faro/map/map_faro.pdf

Sightseeing Highlights

Old Town

The so-called Cidade Velha, Faro's old town, is a well-preserved historic section just to the east of the harbor. Winding cobblestone streets, Moorish-inspired architecture and a definitive sense of traveling back in time will make you want to wander around the 9th-century town for hours on end, marveling the lively mix of styles that has added multiple layers to Faro's character. Tragically, the historic center was burned down by the English troops in 1596 and then rebuilt only to be destroyed once again in the 1755 earthquake.

Remains surviving the Reconquista as well as the devastating earthquake today compete with 19th-century architecture in this delightful maze of alleys. Enter the city thought the significant 18th-century Arco de Villa arch and head towards the Faro Cathedral (Sé) on the orange tree-lined square. The nearby 18th-century Bishop's Palace is a good landmark to walk by before heading to the Municipal Museum where archeological relics unveil the city's long and eventful history.

To exit the historic center, go through the Arco da Porta Nova, a place where the old town meets the water and a departure point for boats heading to the Ria Formosa Natural Park.

Arco de Vila

An 18th-century gateway marking the entrance to the Cidade Velha, the Arco de Vila (Arch of the City) is a neoclassical arch built by the order of the Bishop Francisco Gomes. Designed by Francisco Xavier Fabri and constructed in 1812, the Arco de Vila sits on the site of a former medieval castle gate. With a Moorish portico and a strong brick-vaulted roof, the arch supports the statue of St. Thomas Aquinas (patron saint of Faro). Just above the gateway is the bell tower.

Walk towards the Largo da Sé Street opening up from the gate and you will soon catch a sign of the famous Sé Cathedral as well as the Bishop's Palace – two more landmarks closely most frequently associated with the city.

Cathedral

Largo da Sé, Faro
Tel: +351 289 806 632

Known simply as "Sé" among locals, the 13th-century Faro Cathedral dominates the old town district and is the area's crown jewel. Constructed on the site of a Roman forum turned into a Visigoth cathedral and later into a mosque, the Cathedral was completed in 1251 and its original exterior was clearly Romanesque-Gothic.

Largely rebuilt and renovated after the 1755 earthquake, its tower gate remains an original, as do several chapels. The renovation has resulted in a particularly varied mix of styles, including Baroque, Renaissance and Gothic, perfectly mirroring the city's eclectic collection of period architecture. And though its exterior may not be earth-shattering, the interior definitely is worth a peek; elaborate tiles and gilded carvings as well as a baroque organ are just some of the treasures found on the inside.

If you are on the hunt for spectacular views, make the effort to climb up to the rooftop lookout (*miradouro*) where you also may catch a glimpse of the storks that have made home in the bell towers. From here, you can get a bird's eye view of the typical Portuguese architecture present in Faro, including the iconic red rooftops called *tesouro* as well as the Ria Formosa Park with its magnificent lagoon.

The Cathedral is open daily from 09:00 to 12:30 and from 13:30 to 17:00 while Sunday mass is held at 10:00 and 12:00.

Admission costs €3. Entrance to the cathedral's gilded altar as well as the marbled tombs and chapels costs additional €3.

Bishop's Palace

Largo da Sé 15, Faro

Just opposite the Cathedral is the Bishop's Palace (Paco Episcopal), decorated in multicolored 18-th century hand-painted tiles (*azulejos*). With its red roof, it nowadays is a venue for various religious art exhibitions while its interior is a piece of art itself. The Palace was constructed at the site of the previous Episcopal residence, which was destroyed by the British troops in 1596. Rebuilt after the earthquake, its altarpiece was created in 1786.

Being still the official residence of the Bishop of Faro, the Palace is not open to the public but is nevertheless a lovely landmark to walk by. If your visit coincides with one of the occasional temporary exhibitions held here, you should use the opportunity to take a peek inside.

Municipal Museum of Archeology

Largo Dom Afonso III, Faro
Tel: +351 289 897 400

Housed in one of Portugal's oldest convents – the 16th-century *Convento de Nossa Senhora da Assuncao* - the Municipal Museum of Archeology is one of Algarve's first museums. The museum surveys two millennia's worth of local history and art and is the proud home of the majestic Roman *Mosaic of the Ocean*, depicting Neptune and the Four Winds. Dating to the 3rd century, the mosaic was discovered in 1976 on a building site. A lovely cloister as well as other Roman and Moorish artifacts (both archeological and ecclesiastical) can also be found inside, including many relics excavated at the nearby Estoi site. The famous Faro-born painter Carlos Filipe Porfirio is represented with his moody paintings featuring local legends and religious motifs.

The Museum is open from 09:30 to 17:30 (from 11:30 on weekends) in the summer season and from 10:00 to 18:00 (from 14:00 on weekends) between the months of October and April. Admission fee costs €3 (€1.50 for students).

Ria Formosa Nature Park

Spanning about 60 kilometers of south Portugal's coastline, the Ria Formosa Natural Par was declared one of the country's great natural wonders and is an area of major ecological interest.

A lagoon formed by a sequence of sandpits (*Ilhas*) is the home of wetlands and has been protected since 1987. Unique natural conditions make it a breeding spot for birds, some of which are extremely rare, as well as a variety of marine life. At peak times in the winter season during migration, the park often hosts as many as 20,000 birds, with resident flamingos and the Purple Swamphen being the most recognizable species. A salt production site during Roman times, the landscape of the lagoon changes as one season gives way to the next, with parts of the park sometimes submerged and other times entirely exposed. Today, the area is used for oyster and mussel farming, mostly with the utilization of traditional methods in order to preserve the habitat.

Two peninsulas (Ancao and Cacela) as well as five islands (Barreta, Culatra, Armona, Tavira and Cabanas) make up the Ria Formosa Park. Accessible by small boats from the historic center, the Park can be visited as part of a two and a half hour boat trip (including a 40 minute stay on one of the islands), with prices starting from €10. Full day tours are also available and cost anywhere from €30 to €50 per adult, depending on the tour operator.

Our Lady of Carmel Church & Chapel of Bones

Largo do Carmo, Faro
Tel: +351 289 824 490

Back to the mainland from the Ria Formosa Park and right at the exit of the old town, continue your Faro exploration by moving slightly inland. Just away from the town wall you will soon discover the baroque Igreja de Nossa Senhora do Carmo (Our Lady of Carmel Church). Started in 1713 and completed in 1719 during Joao V's rule, with its façade finished after the historic 1755 earthquake, this Carmelite church is extensively gilded with Brazilian gold in its interior and features imposing twin towers. It also contains significant religious statues, including the nine Triumphal Procession statues by Manuel Martins who also created the Santa Teresa altarpiece.

For those looking for something completely unusual and borderline bizarre, the 19th century Capela dos Ossos (Chapel of Bones) is a true find. The chapel is literally built from and decorated with the bones and skulls of 1,200 monks, all neatly arranged in rows. Completed in 1816, it is a peculiar work of art of the Carmelite monks who built it, inclined to use the remains of their predecessors from a nearby cemetery as a grim reminder of mortality. Entrance fee to this ghoulish chapel costs €1.

Beaches

When you acquainted yourself with Faro's history and culture, the logical choice is to head to one (or more) of the nearby exquisite beaches. Most of the beaches in and around Faro are located on the shallow pits of sand that run along the coastline. This natural landscape creates a wetland lagoon on the internal side, marked by calm and clear waters. The external, ocean-meeting side is somewhat wilder, with waves rolling in from the Atlantic.

Praia de Faro & Ilha de Faro

Faro's beach is a long, gently-sloping stretch of golden sand on Ilha de Faro (Faro Island), some 10 kilometers away from the city. Located on the sandbar that wraps around the coastline, it gets a bit crowded in July and August but nevertheless manages to please all tastes; with gorgeous views, a multitude of facilities and a wide range of entertainment options, it is truly the locals' favorite hangout in the summertime.

To get to the beach, take bus 14 or 16 from across the bus station in the city. The buses run about once every 30 minutes in the summertime and make a stop at the airport. The 45-minute journey itself is irresistibly scenic, particularly when crossing the pine forest region.

Ilha de Barreta/Deserta

Catch a ferry to Ilha de Barreta (also known as Ilha Deserta) to marvel at the long and narrow strip of sand just off the mainland and part of the Ria Formosa National Park. The sandpit that curves around the coast just in front of Faro can be accessed from various points on the mainland. The mind-blowing 10 kilometers of sweeping sands are connected to the wetlands where exotic flamingoes thrive so they provide a different experience from the one usually found on urban purposefully-organized beaches.

Ilha de Barreta is particularly well suited to explorers, with plenty of nature trails available for a change of pace from the more common beach activities. Note that only one restaurant serves the beach, so bringing a snack is recommended.

Vale de Lobo

If you head west of Faro, you will run into the popular Vale do Lobo resort whose dramatic Algarve-typical cliffs provide a stunning change of scenery. A wide beach awaits sun-worshipers, ready to provide its excellent facilities, cafes, bars and restaurants. Vale de Lobo's square (known as Praca) can be found right on the beach while those looking to explore further can head to the golf resort nearby.

Armona

One of the region's most popular beaches, Armona is located east of Faro about 2 kilometers off the Olhao coast and is accessible via ferry from Olhao or Fuseta. Endless sand stretches as far as the eye can reach, inviting leisurely strolls by the water's edge. The sand dunes in the background are home to a number of restaurants and bars while a camping site can also be found nearby.

Living Science Centre

Centro de Ciência Viva, Rua Comandante Francisco Manuel, Faro
Tel: +351 289 890 920
http://www.ccvalg.pt

Faro's Living Science Centre is a great way to spend a day away from the beach, particularly for families with children. A place of learning and discovery, it features interactive exhibitions covering a multitude of areas, such as light, the solar system, and the human body, among others. Children's curious minds will have a chance to look at planets through a telescope or discover marine life with the use of microscopes. Permanent exhibitions dedicated to the sea as well as a flight simulator and astronomical observation sessions are just a few more of the many activities the whole family can engage in during the visit. Opened since 1997, the Living Science Centre is housed in the old fire station near the Manuel Bivar gardens. Entrance costs €3.50 for adults; €1.75 for children under 12.

Estoi & the Milreu Ruins

Just 11 kilometers north of Faro and set in the gorgeous countryside, Estoi is a quaint old town that easily justifies a half-day trip. A bus connects Faro and Estoi and drops visitors off in the main square, close to the 18th century pink rococo Palacio do Visconde de Estoi, nowadays a private palace. The Palace also features beautiful shaded gardens with tropic plants, open to the public.

Stroll downhill from the main square towards the 1st century Milreu Roman site and you will soon find the most compelling reason to visit Estoi - a locality that used to be inhabited between the 2nd and the 10th century, this is Algarve's most impressive and expansive Roman ruins site. Built in the style of a peristyle villa (a columned porch surrounding a court), it features intact columns and original mosaics. A temple originally devoted to the cult of water, then converted to a basilica in the 3rd century AD, is one of the world's oldest churches. The remains of a bathing complex have also withheld the test of time, and feature fish mosaics in the bathrooms and an intricate changing room including a *frigidarium* designed to hold cold water. The villa used to feature an advanced water supply network as well as heated rooms and thermal springs.

Check out the amusing decorations found around the ruins, with fish represented as particularly fat in order to create the optical illusion of movement, testifying to the level of dedication to detail and effort put into the creation of this ancient villa.

Entrance into the ruins costs €2 and they are open from 10:30 to 13:00 and from 14:00 to 18:30 daily between May and September; 09:30 to 13:00 and 14:00 to 17:00 the rest of the year.

Tavira

Another popular day trip out of Faro is Tavira, one of Algarve's prettiest towns. Only 30 kilometers east of Faro and sitting on both sides of the Gilao River, this traditional fishing town was founded as early as 4th century BC and served as a port for trading with North Africa. Tavira is a popular destination not only for its picturesque beauty defined by graceful 18th-century houses, palm trees and low bridges, but also because of the spectacular beach on Ilha de Tavira.

Roman Bridge

Today's bridge being mostly built in 1667 on top of a previous structure, the Roman Bridge was initially constructed during the Islamic al-Andalus rule in Tavira. A vital factor in the defense system of medieval Tavira, it used to have houses erected on it as it connected the two banks of the River Gilao. Collapsing in 1655, it was rebuilt about a decade later, largely featuring today's characteristics.

Partially destroyed once again in the 1989 flood but quickly restored, it is no longer used for motor vehicle traffic and is fully pedestrianized, thus inviting a leisurely stroll.

An interesting detail worth noting is the fact that the river to the west of the bridge is known as Gilao while the very same river goes by the name Sequa to east; the reason can be found in a complex local legend that involves two lovers who had tragically drowned on either side of the bridge.

Tavira Island

Easily accessible from the town of Tavira via a ferry, the Ilha de Tavira (Tavira Island) stretches out towards the southwest and is a giant 14-kilometers-long beach with spectacular dunes in the background. Its width varies between 150 meters and 1 kilometer, making it seem truly endless at times. Likely one of Algarve's best beaches, it is typically flocked to in the summertime but it is relatively easy to steer clear of the crowds on such a large stretch. Even naturists can find spots specifically designed for them on Ilha de Tavira. Bars and restaurants cater to travelers' every needs as does the variety of beach sceneries – those looking for more tranquil waters should head to the lagoon-facing side, while those not intimidated by waves will delight if they choose the Atlantic-facing orientation.

Tavira's blue flag beach can be accessed from the mainland (Quatro Aguas) via frequent ferries (from €1.50 round trip) or water taxis (from €20). If you are charmed by the beach and wish to spend a night on Tavira Island, look into the camping site under the pine trees – the only available overnight accommodation on the Ilha de Tavira.

Vilamoura

Vilamoura is a luxurious tourist resort and the largest complex of its kind in Europe. Stretching over an area of 20 km², it was built with a purpose to accommodate a variety of tastes and is most notably known for its marina, golf course complexes and a dense population of hotels. For those looking for a bit of history and culture, the nearby Cerro da Vila ruins are a logical choice as they are one of the most significant archeological sites in the country.

Vilamoura is located 23 kilometers west of Faro and is accessible via bus (€4 one way) or taxi (starting from €27 one way).

Vilamoura Marina

Vilamoura
Tel: +351 289 310 560
http://www.marinadevilamoura.com/en

The main center of activity in Vilamoura, the marina is alive with restaurants, bars and shops, some of which are decidedly upscale. This is Portugal's largest marina and is sure to keep you entertained for hours. Peaceful during the day and pulsing with life at night, it attracts everyday folk as well as the wealthy and the popular.

With a capacity to berth more than 1,000 boats, it sees a lot of yacht traffic and also provides options for chartering boats.

Water sports activities are frequently organized as well, and include deep-sea fishing, cruises and scuba diving. The marina was recently voted Best Portuguese Marina for 2013 and certainly makes Vilamoura a particularly cosmopolitan destination along the Algarve coast.

Cerro da Vila

Avenida Cerro Da Vila, 8125-403 Vilamoura
Tel: +351 289 312 153

Just steps from the marina, the Cerro da Vila ruins with leftovers from ancient civilizations are a great way to spend a few more hours in Vilamoura. The particular site has been occupied since the Bronze Age but the earliest settlers were the Romans who have left an unmistakable mark on the area, mostly between the 2nd and 3rd century AD. Cerro da Vila then belonged to the Ossonoba province and served the lands around the settlement with its port.

Remnants of a rustic mansion (Roman Villa), public bath-houses and fish salting tanks can be found on this ruins complex, as well as foundations of a tower used for burials. The area is nowadays an archeological site of immense importance in Algarve. A museum has been created within the complex, to serve as a guide to visitors wanting to further explore the significance of the site. The ruins are open from 10:00 to 13:00 and from 16:00 to 21:00 in the summertime. Between the months of November and April you can visit the Cerro da Villa from 09:30 to 12:30 or from 14:00 to 18:00. Entrance to the site costs €5.

Recommendations for the Budget Traveller

Places To Stay

Casa d'Alagoa Hostel

Praca Alexandre Herculano 27, 8000-160 Faro
Tel: +351 289 813 252
http://farohostel.com/

If you don't mind staying in a hostel, consider the historical Casa d'Alagoa – an affordable accommodation in central Faro that is sure to please a range of tastes.

Both private and shared rooms are available in this excellently located and clean hostel just across the Alagoa garden, with great connections to Faro's beaches. One can also easily reach the historic Arco da Vila in only 5 minutes on foot.

The high-ceilinged rooms come equipped with Wi-Fi, a buffet breakfast and the use of a convenient communal kitchen. Laundry services and bike rentals are also available through the staff reception desk.

At the start of the summer season, private bathroom double rooms start from €48 per night, including breakfast while beds in shared dormitories start from €17 per night.

Hotel Ibis Faro

Estrada Nacional 125, 8000-770 Faro
Tel: +351 289 893 800
http://www.ibis.com/gb/hotel-1593-ibis-faro/index.shtml

Just two kilometers from Faro's center, the Hotel Ibis Faro – part of the Ibis chain of hotels – is perfectly located for easy access to the nearby beaches, the Ria Formosa Natural Park and the historic center with its landmarks. The hotel's 81 rooms all include Wi-Fi access and are simply decorated, with private bathrooms and A/C. An outdoor swimming pool and a bar with a terrace are available for hotel's guests as is the private parking. Golf lovers should know that the nearest course is merely 10 kilometers away.

Double rooms in the early summer season (June) start from €49 per night, with an optional breakfast price of €6 per person per night.

Hotel Adelaide

Rua Cruz das Mestras n 9, 8000-261 Faro
Tel: +351 289 802
http://www.adelaideresidencial.net

For another affordable option in central Faro, travelers should look into the 2-star Hotel Adelaide – a 19-room hotel within walking distance of the Faro bus station and the marina. Rooms are bright and offer free Wi-Fi and air-conditioning while the hotel also has a restaurant serving daily buffet breakfast. Shared kitchen facilities are also available for use by hotel's guests.

The 19 double rooms in the Adelaide are available at rates starting at €50 per night in the mid-season, breakfast included.

Hotel Faro

Praça D. Francisco Gomes, N 2, 8000 -168 Faro
Tel: +351 289 830 830
http://www.hotelfaro.pt/

If you are looking for affordable accommodation right in the middle of Faro's center, look no further than Hotel Faro, a 4-star choice overlooking the old town and the marina. Large and bright rooms come with cable TV, a minibar and private bathrooms, while some also include balconies. A buffet breakfast is optional and a restaurant on the rooftop serves Portuguese cuisine as well.

Prices for one of Hotel Faro's 90 rooms start from €75 for a double room in the mid-season, breakfast included.

Quinta dos Poetas, Hotel Rural Olhao

Sítio da Arretorta, 8700-180 Olhão
Tel: + 351 289 990 990
http://www.quintadospoetas.com/

Outside Faro and in located in Olhao's countryside, the Hotel Rural Quinta dos Poetas is set against picturesque scenery. Providing 22 rooms with private balconies, air-condition and wooden furniture, the hotel also offers a pool, a fitness room and a local cuisine restaurant.

 Renting a bicycle to explore the nearby Ria Formosa is easy and is a great option for nature lovers. Free private parking is also available on the hotel's grounds.

Double rooms with breakfast in the early summer season start at €75 per night.

Places to Eat & Drink

Columbus Cocktail and Wine Bar

Praca Dom Francisco Gomes, 13, Faro
Tel: +351 917 762 22
http://www.barcolumbus.pt/

Head here right before dinner for a glass of perfect sangria or for a delicious cocktail afterwards. Columbus Bar, located just across from the marina, is a favorite with locals and tourists alike and serves a wide range of excellent cocktails on a nice terrace.

A stylish bar inside is another option for visitors and the attentive staff also serves delicious tapas. Cocktails cost about €6 and some of the more popular ones include the Strawberry Daiquiri and the Cosmopolitan. The clientele is varied at this popular bar, with hordes of repeat visitors coming in from all over Algarve.

Tasca do Ricky

Rua do Forno, N021, Faro
Tel: +351 919 111 057

This typical Portuguese tasca (small restaurant) is a great choice for a filling and affordable lunch, with a large portion main dish, dessert, drink and coffee setting you back a mere €6. Home-cooked food and a very friendly service are Ricky's trademark as the owner is known to personally greet patrons at the door. Don't ask for a menu; simply follow his instructions as he guides you through what is at its best and freshest that day. The restaurant is closed on Sunday evenings.

Jamie's Faro

Largo de Sao Pedro 54, Faro
Tel: +351 961 480 083
http://www.jamiesfaro.com/

Definitely one of the more popular restaurants in the city, Jamie's Faro offers excellent value for money. Located near the Chapel of Bones, it features a lovely terrace providing a relaxed setting for al-fresco dining as well as impeccable service by the courteous staff. The menu of the day costs just under €9 and includes a dish (selected from four options), drink and coffee. Try the risotto with grilled stuffed chicken and the exquisite chocolate mousse and don't skip a glass of the excellent house white wine.

Adega Nova

Rua Francisco Barreto, 24, Faro
Tel: +351 289 813 433

The rustic and informal Adega Nova serves quality food which changes ever so slightly day by day. Try the Algarve cheese as a starter and continue on to sample delightful fresh seafood such as octopus with rice or the mixed seafood skewer (€13). Wash it all down with the young sparkling wine Vinho Verde as you chat with the locals sitting on the next table for a true cultural immersion experience.

Atelier de Comida Sto Antonio

Largo de Camoes 23/24, Faro
Tel: +351 289 802 148
http://www.atelierdecomida.com/

Excellent food and wine await you in the Atelier de Comida Sto Antonio and you will soon realize that the restaurant is packed with locals – always a good sign. The backyard is a lovely setting for outdoor dining in the summertime. Competitively priced and delicious dishes include monkfish shish-kebab (€12.50), sauteed sea bream (€12.50), bacon-wrapped sea bass (€13.50) and pork tenderloin with clams (€11.50), to name just a few. Takeaway options are also available, with the soup of the day particularly well priced at only €1.

Places To Shop

Forum Algarve

Forum Algarve EN 125 Km 103, Faro
Tel: +351 289 889 300
http://www.forumalgarve.net/

The Forum Algarve shopping mall, located on the main
EN125 road, has a wide selection of shops, restaurants
and cafes and an open air central square. Shopping
aficionados will delight at the more than 100 stores
spanning a wide range of goods (including fashion,
cosmetics, home ware, books, gifts and a good selection of
services). There is also a cinema complex in the Forum, a
large supermarket as well as over 20 different restaurant
and café establishments. The Forum Algarve is easibly
accessible by public minibus transport which runs every
15 minutes.

Mercado Municipal de Faro

Largo Doutor Francisco Sá Carneiro, Faro
Tel: +351 289 897 250
http://www.mercadomunicipaldefaro.pt

If you are on the hunt for fresh produce or simply want to mingle with the locals, head to the Mercado Municipal where countless stalls will delight you with the freshest of ingredients and their varied offerings. The indoor market is a heaven for foodies and those looking to stock up on food gifts (such as salty olives and cured meats) all at amazingly low prices. For a sweet treat while you shop, try the delicious custard tarts.

Carminho

Rua Santo António 29, Faro
Tel: +351 289 826 522

Most of Faro's shopping can be found along the Rua Santo Antonio street right in the center of the city. If you have souvenir shopping to do, check out the Carminho store where handicrafts and some traditional Portuguese attire await you. Traditional painted *azulejos*, tableware, embroidery and items made of copper are just a few more of the products on sale at the well-stocked Carminho.

Garrafeira Rui

Praça Ferreira de Almeida, 28, 8000 Faro
Tel: +351 289 822 803

If you have, like many others before you, fallen in love with delicious Portuguese wines, head to the Garrafeira Rui – Faro's best known wine shop. Here you can stock up on local wines and port as well as purchase local delicacies, such as sausages, cheeses and sweets. The store is open Monday to Saturday from 08:00 to 20:00.

Estoi Flea Market

If you can time your visit to Estoi to coincide with the 2nd Sunday of the month, take advantage of the large open air market where traders from all over the region congregate to sell produce, clothing, antiques and a large selection of handmade crafts. Items worth hunting for here include hats and baskets woven from palm leaves – one of Algarve's most popular souvenirs.

The Algarve

The Algarve is located on the south coast of Portugal and is the country's most popular vacation destination. With two hundred kilometres of sandy beaches and delightful seaside, the Algarve is surprisingly cheap, very safe and rich in culture and diversity.

The sunbathed Portuguese coast is conveniently located just 2-4 hours flight from the colder climates of Northern Europe. The waters of the Algarve are ideal for swimming, and many of the beaches feature interesting coves, cliffs and other rock formations to provide interesting and unique sights both above and below the water line.

There are a number of interesting limestone caves and lagoons that are well worth exploring. Best known of these is the extended lagoon known as Ria Formosa.

Water sports are not the only activities to pursue, when on vacation here. The region has great facilities for a number of other sporting activities, such as horseriding, tennis, cycling and golf.

The Algarve has a number of superb golf courses, reckoned to be among the finest on the European continent. The golf course at Vilamoura has hosted the Portuguese Masters Golf Tournament for several years, attracting the world's top ranking players each year. This location was designed by the American legend, Arnold Palmer, who was nicknamed 'The King' in his heyday and is still considered to be one of the Big Three of golf. Elsewhere, you will find courses designed by greats such as Nick Faldo.

The region of the Algarve has seen settlement since Neolithic times. As the Phoenicians ventured throughout the Mediterranean, they established ports around 1000 BC. In its long and extensive history, the Algarve region has seen occupation by Phoenicians, Romans, Visigoths and Moors. Even after the re-conquest by Christian forces, raids from Africa remained a problem till the 1500s.

It was largely from a need to protect the integrity of its coastal settlements that the Portuguese began to embark on a campaign of conquest in the Northwestern parts of Africa. This brought the country both prestige and considerable wealth through trade, but in 1755 a large earthquake wreaked devastation throughout Portugal. The Algarve did not escape its impact and for this reason, very few complete buildings dating before the disaster survived.

Culture

Today's Algarve is friendly and a mainstream tourist destination and the lifestyle here is relaxed and easy-going. Fishing has played a large role in the local economy and continues to do so. For this reason, the traditional cuisine shows a strong preference towards seafood. A fisherman's boat is his pride and joy, which often shows in the decoration lavished upon it. Religion plays an important role and well over 90 percent of the inhabitants are Catholic.

Many local traditions have remained virtually unchanged for centuries, yet there is a sizable population of English-speaking residents, both temporary and semi-permanent. The lifestyle is relaxed and tranquil.

While many towns have developed to fully-fledged resort locations, some of the village charm remains intact in the cobbled streets, the historic district and in the regular markets, sometimes referred to as gypsy markets.

In the summer months, the region hosts various cultural and religious festivals, including the famous one in Loule, an International Music Festival and a National Folklore Festival that includes events in different locations across the Algarve. Alcoutim showcases local crafts in a Handicraft Festival in July, while Cacela Velha showcases the Muslim heritage in an event called Moorish Nights. Basketmaking and pottery are local crafts.

Location & Orientation

The Algarve is in the southwestern part of the Iberian Peninsula. It is a narrow strip of land, which occupies the entire southern coast of Portugal, from the border with Spain in the east and past the southernmost tip of Europe at Cape St Vincent. From there, it sweeps northwards on the western side for some 52 km. At its widest segments, the Algarve reaches about 36 km inland. It is bounded by the Alentejo region to the north.

Much of the coast of the Algarve is characterized by the combination of attractive beaches flanked by dramatic cliff faces. Towards the northern part, the land steadily rises in ranges of gently rounded hills and mountains.

The region is serviced by Faro airport, which connects to various major destinations around the world. A railway system runs roughly parallel to the coast, reaching from Vila Real do Santo António in the east to Lagos in the Western Algarve. This rail network also connects the region to the rest of Portugal via Lisbon.

By road, the Algarve was bisected by the EN 125, a road that ran from East to West along the entire coast. In recent years, this has been replaced by a newer motorway, the A22. A network of bus services connect different parts of the Algarve.

Climate & When to Visit

The Algarve enjoys a pleasant, sunny climate that is ideal for beach and outdoor activities. The warmest months are July and August, when maximum temperatures hover around 28 to 29 degrees Celsius and nights can be expected to be fairly warm, with minimums of around 23 to 24 being typical.

In the winter months of December and January, day temperatures will average around 16 to 17 degrees Celsius, with nightly temperatures dropping to between 8 and 9 degrees Celsius.

These are averages for the whole region and the temperatures in individual towns and cities may vary slightly, although not by a wide margin. Faro, for example, sees average summer highs of up to 29 degrees and on individual days, the mercury may rise even higher to reach above 30 degrees Celsius. The sea temperature is typically around 20 degrees Celsius in summer and it may drop to around 16 degrees Celsius in winter.

Rainfall is scarce and can mainly be expected in the winter months between November and March. Even at the height of winter, you will still see sunny days for much of the time.

The best off-season periods to visit will be during the latter part of spring or the earliest period of autumn. In May, the temperatures average between 22 degrees Celsius in the daytime, dropping to around 13 degrees Celsius at night. Even the month of October still sees averages between 23 and 15 degrees Celsius.

Sightseeing Highlights

Lagos

The town of Lagos had been settled for over 2000 years, but its golden era had been the years between 1420 and 1460, when it played a huge part in altering the fortunes of the Algarve and Portugal as a whole. Lagos had been inhabited by Carthaginians, Romans, Visigoths, Byzantines and Moors, but it is best remembered as the location from which the illustrious Age of Discovery was launched.

Prince Henry the Navigator, the third son of King John of Portugal, was born in 1394. From a relatively young age, he was motivated by the possibility of rich trade on the African continent, especially after the Portuguese capture of Ceuta, a port in Morocco that had served as a base for Barbary raids into Portugal.

When Henry was appointed as the Governor of Algarve, he based himself on the Sagres Peninsula and a number of innovations in sea travel resulted, such as the development of a lighter vessel called a caravel and new insights on cartography.

Gil Eanes, an early Portuguese explorer who was first to round the West African peninsula of Cape Bojador in 1435, was a native of Lagos. This early achievement in the service of Prince Henry the Navigator played an important role in later voyages of the Age of Discovery.

Both Gil Eanes and Prince Henry the Navigator are honored with statues, Henry's being in the vicinity of Praça da República. Other statues in Lagos are that of São Gonçalo on Avenida dos Descobrimentos, honoring the region's only homegrown saint and Dom Sebastiao on the Main Square.

Some notable buildings of Lagos are the Governor's Castle or Castelo dos Governadores, with some walls dating back to Moorish times and Forte da Ponta da Bandeira.

Today, Lagos is a popular stop for tourists. It has several beautiful and accessible beaches. Meia Praia with its beach bars and boardwalk is popular with tourists. The crowded Praia da Batata is conveniently located right by the town center and offers conveniences such as sun beds, water sporting opportunities and the views of Forte Ponta da Bandeira. Praia da Dona Ana can be reached by a series of wooden steps and is surrounded by majestic cliff and rock formations. Another beach worth a visit, not only for its unusual rock structures, but also the surrounding flora and impressive caves nearby, is Ponta da Piedade.

The marina at Lagos offers the opportunity for boat tours and dolphin watching. A boat trip also enables a unique view of Ponta da Piedada's unusual features and its lighthouse. Lovers of water sport can enjoy activities such as diving, kayaking or sailing, while Lagos also has excellent facilities for tennis, Go-karting, land sailing, golf and horse-riding. There is a Slide and Splash water park a mere 20 minutes away from Lagos.

Antigo Mercado de Escravos (Slave Market)

Praca do Infante Dom Henriques, Lagos, Portugal

Now a small art gallery, this was once the site where fierce trade in human stock took place during Portugal's Age of Discovery.

It had been the first place where slaves were auctioned and some of the exhibits include skeletons, artwork and craft items made by Africans who were brought here to be traded. Admission is € 1.50.

Church of St. Sebastian (Igreja de Sao Sebastiao)

Rua Conselheiro Joaquim Machado, Lagos 8600, Portugal

The church's most memorable feature must surely be the ossuary, which features various bones and skulls embedded into the walls. Although only three storeys high, the bell tower gives an elevated view of the historic town center, the beach and Bensafrim River. Admission is € 2.

Church of St. Anthony (Igreja de Santo Antonio)

Rua General Alberto da Silveira, Lagos 8600-594, Portugal
Tel: 282 762 301

The detailed golden artwork featured within the church is one of its attractions, but these days it functions more as a museum than a place of worship.

The collection on display includes artwork, engravings and even ancient Roman artefacts. Some of its art treasures are specifically dedicated to St Anthony. Admission is € 3.

Zoo Lagos

Quinta Figueiras - Sítio do Medronhal
Barão de S. João
Lagos - Algarve – Portugal 8600
Tel: 282 680 100
http://www.zoolagos.com

Lagos Zoo strives to combine conservation with education and houses its animals within beautiful and environmentally suitable habitats. Some of the residents include gibbons, lemurs, marmosets, bobcats, prairie dogs, a pygmy hippo, meerkat, wallabi and various species of cranes, swans, hornbills and turkeys. There are also animals such as horses, ponies, donkeys, pot-bellied pigs, goats, guinea pigs, llamas and a petting zoo for kids. The focus is on smaller animals, but the grounds also includes a variety of flora from around the world. Admission is €14 for adults.

Tavira

The history of Tavira dates back about 4000 years, to 2000 BC and it is easy to see why. The Gilão River forms a pleasant backdrop to this town's scenery, but must have served as a trade artery in earlier times.

The market hall is now the setting of several shops and restaurants and a prominade with attractive pavillion and shaded benches for a moment's relaxation.

A low, arched structure known widely as the Roman bridge has on closer inspection been revealed to be of Moorish manufacture, dating back to the 12th century. Nowadays it is a pedestrian only crossing. The surrounding architecture dates back to the 18th century, after the earthquake of 1755. The bridge also includes a monument for the fallen heroes of Portugal's struggle for independence between 1383 and 1385.

A few kilometers outside Tavira you will find Pego do Inferno. This relaxing spot in nature is basically a waterfall that empties into a pool at Santo Estêvã. Another attraction of Tavira is the Rio Formosa with one of its barrier islands being Tavira Island. Its wide beach area is regarded as one of the best beaches of the Algarve, and can be reached by ferry. The island also has camping facilities and restaurants.

Tavira Castle

The partial remains of the Moorish castle makes an imposing sight in Tavira's historical section. The first fortification to occupy the site may date back as far as 800 BC, to the time of the Phoenicians. Captured from the Moors in 1239, the castle was gifted to the Order of the Knights of Santiago in 1342, but returned to the King after three decades.

It was rebuilt towards the end of the thirteenth century as a strategy against increased pirate activity. Unfortunately, it suffered serious damage during the earthquake of 1755.

What remains of the fort are three walls, two square towers and one octagon-shaped tower. A small garden can be found within the courtyard. The site is allegedly haunted by the spirit of a young Moorish woman who had been the daughter of the last Muslim governor, Aben-Fabila. The castle's remaining features command a great view of Tavira. Admission is free.

Portimão

Portimão is located where the Arade River empties into the sea, making it the ideal location for a port, especially to a region as focused on maritime affairs as the Algarve. The marina has mooring space for well over 600 vessels. Here too, you will find shops, restaurants, bars and prime residential real estate. Two fortresses on opposite banks of the Arade, Santa Catarina and São Joãio were constructed in the 1500s to protect port interests. Another guardian is the lighthouse on the Ferragudo Peninsula.

The city boasts one of the most popular beaches of the Algarve, Praia da Rocha. With excellent facilities, it can get quite crowded at the height of summer. It carries Blue Flag status, as does several other beaches in the area, such as Praia do Vau, Praia do AlvorPoente and Praia dos TrêsIrmãos, which is rendered distinct by a striking rock formation nearby.

To catch a glimpse of the old ways, visit the traditional fishing village of Ferragudo, which is just opposite the river from Portimão. A charming place to pause is in the old district of Portimão is the fountain near the old market hall. The area is a stop on the Lisbon to Dakar Rally. In summer, Portimão hosts a beach soccer challenge.

Faro

Although few buildings in Faro survived the earthquake of 1755 intact, the city does feature ruins of both Arab and Roman descent. The older part of town still has remnants of the Roman walls and the open square preserves the layout of a Roman forum.

In the oldest district, you could explore Faro's marina or Jardim Manuel Bivar, a botanical garden where visitors and locals enjoy strolling. Here too, you will find a popular pedestrian shopping region. The district features various townhouses in the Jugendstil architectural style.

Considering the region's illustrious maritime heritage, the Naval Museum is certainly worth a visit. The church of NossoSenhora is famous for its style of gold-leaf covered woodwork and also the Chapel of Bones, which holds the earthly remains of around 1200 monks.

Faro serves as administrative capital and is located near the region's main airport. It has also been the seat of the Bishop of the Algarve since the latter part of the 1500s, only a few decades after it officially became a city in 1540. As many religious buildings in the Algarve, the Sé Cathedral still preserves elements of the mosque that once occupied its place.

The beachfront area of Faro forms part of the Ria Formosa. The main beach area, Praia do Faro-Mar, is accessible via a bridge. Another beach, Praia da Barreta, can only be reached by ferry.

Faro Archaeological Museum

Tel: 289 803 604

The Faro Archaeological Museum is located within a convent constructed in the early 1500s. The architecture is in itself something to admire. Collected within you will discover various finds from the area, including Roman mosaics, sculptures and relics of religious significance. The paintings exhibited date mainly from the 16th and 17th century and include works of Portuguese and Italian origin. There are also objects from the Moorish period.

Igreja do Carmo Church / Capela dos Ossos (Chapel of Bones)

Within the chapel of bones you will find row upon row of skulls. This ornate but grisly decoration is provided by the remains of monks who had been buried in the cemetery that once occupied this site. It was built in 1816.

Estoi Palace

Rua de Sao Jose, 8005 Estoi
Tel: 289 990 150

Commissioned by José Francisco da Silva, the Viscount of Estoi in the late 1800s, the lavish palace was eventually completed in 1909. It features the Rococo style, but also includes beautiful tileworkThe site is currently being transformed into a hotel.

Milreu

Off the N2, about 20 minutes out of Faro, Estoi

The ruins at Milreu date back to Roman times. The complex includes a temple, winepress and baths as well as an extensive plumbing system.

Water is a recurrent theme in the decorative art, of which the preserved fish mosaics are a good example. In the 3rd century its function shifted from villa to farm. Towards the 6th century, it became a church and after the 10th century it served as Muslim cemetery.

A visitor's center near the actual digs displays how the Romans lived.

Admission to the site is €2.

Ria Formosa

The Ria Formosa is an extended lagoon created by a system of barrier islands and peninsulas stretching from Manta Rota to Garrão, a distance of about 60 km.

Punctuated by a series of sand dunes, sand bars and isles, this area was formed with the oceanic upheavals of the earthquake of 1755. There are five main islands, namely Faro, Barreta, Culatra, Armona and Tavira.

The area is utilized in various ways by the Algarve people. Salt deposits are harvested near Tavira, as the region is relatively uncontaminated by pollutants. Other products of the area are fish and shellfish. The region accounts for 80 percent of Portugal's exports in clams.

The maze-like formations have six points of entry towards the beach region of which five are natural. These features offer protection to a variety of species, making it an ideal breeding ground. Endangered species, such as sea horses and chameleons also find sanctuary here.

Due to the large number of migratory and nesting water birds such as flamingo and heron found here, it is popular with bird watching enthusiasts. Another native of this territory is the Portuguese water dog. These friendly animals often served as invaluable aids to fishermen, but faced extinction in recent years. Fortunately their numbers have recovered somewhat.

The Ria Formosa has been a National Park since 1987. The region combines duneland, marshland and woodland and includes a number of interesting hiking trails. Faro Island is accessible by road and there is a regular bus service to the island. Armona Island and Tavira Island boasts some excellent beaches and can be reached by ferry or water taxi.

Vilamoura

The resort of Vilamoura encompasses a casino and marina, a series of superior beaches, and a great selection of shops, restaurants and nightspots. The nearby vicinity offers a variety of outdoor activities which include horse-riding, tennis, water sports and golf.

The facilities on offer for the golfing enthusiasts are of a particularly high standard. Vilamoura lies just off the Golden Triangle, a region well known for its luxury housing and outstanding golf courses. The Portuguese Masters Golf Tournament is held in Vilamoura.

From the marina, you can organize leisurely coastal cruises or big game fishing excursions. There are plenty of opportunities for hiking or cycling in the area as well.

Albufeira

Within a few decades, Albufeira grew from humble fishing village to populous resort town. Its premier beach, Praia dos Pescadores is located near the historical part of town and still has a section set aside for fishing boats. The other beach, Praia do Túnel is named after its access point - a tunnel through which all beachgoers must pass.

From the modern sculptures incorporated in several of the town's traffic circles to the picturesque square of the old district, Albufeira is easy on the eye.

Two main commercial arteries of the town are Rua 5 de Outubro and Ave Dr. Francisco SáCarneiro, also known as The Strip, which is favored by English-speaking visitors and residents. As Albufeira is a popular tourist destination, English is often heard, seen and used.

A colorful feature of Albufeira is its marina. The surrounding buildings are painted in a combination of orange, pink, green amd blue. It was created through the demolition of a natural rock wall. An important landmark of Albufeira, its clocktower, once served a very different function. It had been part of a castle.

Monchique

Unlike the coastal regions, Monchique is still relatively undiscovered by tourist trends. It is located between two hills, the Picota and the Fóia and provides a pleasant mix of narrow, cobbled lanes full of character and beautiful scenery.

Nearby is Fóia, at 902m, the highest point of the Serra de Monchique hills. It is the site of a radar station. The view here is very wide, including sights such as Cape St. Vincent, the southern most point of Europe, the city Faro and Serra da Arrabida.

Surrounding features of the area include an aqueduct, waterfalls and impressive granite structures.

The most striking element of the Monchique central square is an old Moorish water wheel. Fans of ceramic art may wish to visit Casa da Nogueira, the birthplace of LeonelTeo, a Portuguese exponent of this art form. The Quinta de São Bento, formerly a summer retreat for the royal family, now serves as hotel and restaurant.

There is also a sulphuric hot spring, Fonte Santa with the adjacent spa at Caldas de Monchique. This has been known since the Roman era. A Franciscan monastery from the 1600s nestles near the town. The area is famous for Medronho, a local spirit distilled from arbutus berries.

Silves

Silves was probably founded around 1000 BC and was utililized by both the Romans and the Visigoths during their reign of the region. Via the Arade River, and its proximity to Portimão, Silves grew to an important trading town. The Moors raised Silves to the status of capital, but were unable to hold it for longer than a few centuries.

Several towns and cities in the Algarve possess a crossing known as Ponte Romana or the Old Roman Bridge and Silves is no different. The design, composed of several low arches, is fairly typical, but it is more likely that it was constructed in the Middle Ages, despite the name. Today it serves pedestrian traffic only. A small market trades nearby.

Various buildings in Silves can be admired for the tiled facades often associated with Portuguese architecture. Silves Cathedral, with its gothic doors dates back to the 13th century, when the reconquesta of Portugal brought new religious fervor to the Algarve. A later church, the Igreja da Misericórdia, displays a later variation on the gothic theme. This church also has an art gallery.

Silves Castle

R. do Castelo, Silves, Algarve, Portugal

Silves Castle occupies a prime strategic position near the mouth of the Arade River.

This site may have served as fortification as far back as the time of the Romans, but the present castle is believed to date back to the period just prior to the Moorish conquest, most likely around 715. It has a lively history. After the Moorish conquest, it was briefly taken by Fernando I, King of Leon in 1060, before falling a second time to the Moors.

In 1189, a Portuguese Christian army, aided by Crusaders from England, Germany and Flanders regained Silves Castle for King Sancho I of Portugal. Later Moorish attempts to occupy the castle proved unsuccessful. Sancho disarmed the structure, but it was rebuilt and refurnished during the mid to late 1300s. The earthquake of 1755 wrought significant damage to the castle, but it was still declared a national monument in 1910, being the largest castle of its kind in the Algarve.

The layout includes a citadel, battlement walls and a total of eleven square towers. It is made of a combination of red sandstone and taipa, a mixture often used in Moorish structures. There is a sad legend associated with the El MouraEncantada, where a Moorish princess allegedly still mourns her lost sweetheart.

From its elevated location, the castle ramparts command a spectacular view of the rest of Silves. Admission is € 2.50.

Cork Museum

Fábrica do Inglés, Rua Gregório Mascarenhas
Phone: 242 440 480

Silves falls within the region where cork is cultivated and processed and an interesting stop to make is the cork museum. This was an important industry of Silves up to the beginning of the 20th century and once employed thousands of townsfolk in multiple factories.

Archaeological Museum

14 Rua das Portas de Loulé, 8300-139 Silves
Tel: 282 444 832

Since the earliest human activity within this region dates back to prehistoric times, there are many interesting Palaeolithic and Neolithic finds on display here, alongside artefacts from Roman, Moorish and more recent history. The remaining wall of a well from the Middle Ages forms part of the building. Admission is € 2.

Loule

Loule occupies an expanse of land that begins at the Algarve coast and stretches up to 12 km inland. It combines healthy commercial growth with the old world beauty of its historic district where reminders of Moorish architecture can still be seen.

One of the city's big attractions is its annual festival. In February, crowds line the street to watch a parade of colorful floats and super sized mannikins. The event attracts many visitors.

A harmonious, but modern water feature decorates the Largo de Gago Coutinho or central square of Loule. In this area you will also find the market hall, an elegant building of Moorish origin. This is the scene of a weekly Saturday market where lace, copperware, leather ware and earthenware can be purchased. By comparison, the town hall is a building of simple geometric features.

One of the town's better known residents was the Portuguese poet, António Aleixo. Although unassuming, his thoughts and writings left an intellectual legacy that is not only recognized in his own country, but also in other Portuguese speaking nations, such as Brazil. He spent his last years in Loule and today bronze statue of Aleixo sits at a table opposite the Calcinha café, as he often did in life.

Three towers and some walls are what remains of the town's Moorish castle, which dates back to the 13th century. It now functions as a museum and houses the town archives.

Some of the key buildings of Loule attest to a policy of reclaiming and recycling its history. The arched Portas do Céu or town gate was once part of the castle complex. Igreja Matriz de São Clemente or the town church was built in the 13th century, incorporating the portal of a mosque that had once occupied the site and it includes a separate belfry of granite that was originally a Moorish minaret.

Convento do Espírito Santo

Rua Vice- Almirante Cândido dos Reis, Loulé
Tel: 289 400 600

Although built in the 17th century, the Monastery of the Holy Spirit suffered significant damage during the devastating earthquake that hit Portugal in 1755.The epicenter struck Lisbon, but its impact was also felt in the Algarve and beyond. The building was reconstructed in the 18th century. It now hosts an art collection.

Neolithic Sites

The Iberian Peninsula is rich with the remains of Neolithic culture and the Algarve boasts several locations with interesting finds. At Alacar, various ancient funeral sites have been uncovered. The most striking of these, known as Monument 7, is a well-preserved cairn of stones arranged in a circular tholos shape.

Montes dos Amantes has a different type of heritage from the past. The site is a garden of menhirs, dating back to between 3,000 and 4,000 BC. It is believed that they originated from another location, but were transported here.The sizes vary and some include decorative details. There are also footprints of early humans preserved in stone. The site is located between Vila do Bispo and Sagres.

There is a particularly extensive collection of menhirs near Praia da Ingrina. They are believed to be associated with the fertility cults of the prehistoric inhabitants.

Recommendations for the Budget Traveller

Places to Stay

While the accommodation tariffs in the Algarve is generally very affordable, it should be born in mind that many hotels add a special levy for a stay of less than three nights.

Tivoli Lagos Hotel

Rua Antonio Crisogono Santos, Lagos 8600-678, Portugal
http://www.algarvetivolilagos.com/

The Tivoli Hotel in Lagos offers you the opportunity to enjoy a variety of conveniences at affordable prices. There are three restaurants, with different specialities as well as a Pool Bar to provide refreshments. Other on-site entertainment includes a games room with facilities for table tennis, darts, cards, snooker and chess, a sauna, a Jacuzzi, three outdoor swimming pools, plus a heated indoor one and also a fitness center.

Some of the nearby attractions for visitors include Lagos Zoo, Aqualand and the Slide & Splash water park. Meia Praia beach is right by the hotel. Facilities are wheelchair friendly. Rooms include a safe, a mini-bar, air-conditioning, satellite TV and Wifi Internet. Breakfast is included in the price. Accommodation begins at €58 a night.

Casa das Oliveiras

Montes da Vala,
Silves 8300-044, Portugal
Tel: 282 342 115
http://www.casa-das-oliveiras.com/

Casa das Oliveiras is a small, but highly rated guesthouse in Silves. The garden provides a tranquil spot to relax amid olive trees and cork oaks. There is also a pool and a terrace where breakfast is served. A well-equipped kitchenette is available for use by the guests. Casa das Oliveiras offers facilities for table tennis, satellite TV and free Wifi. All rooms include a bathroom. Accommodation varies between € 27 and € 65.

Hotel Porta Nova

Rua Antonio Pinheiro,
Tavira 8800-323, Portugal
Tel: 282 423 770

Hotel Porta Nova is conveniently located near the historical district, public transport and plenty of bars and restaurants. All rooms feature en-suite bathroom facilities and include a mini-bar, safe and satellite TV. There are swimming pools, a game room and a well-equipped sauna that offers steam, Jacuzzi and massage services.

The reception area has free Wifi Internet. The hotel reception is also a great source of tourist information. Accommodation begins at €20 a night.

Hotel Sol Algarve

Rua Infante D. Henrique, 52,
Faro 8000-363, Portugal
Tel: 289 895 700
http://www.hotelsolalgarve.com/

When Hotel Sol Algarve was enlarged in 2004, its
grounds were found to contain the remains of Roman
ruins. The hotel is located near the train station and the
historical district and boasts a friendly, attractive interior.
All rooms include en-suite bathrooms, air conditioning,
cable TV and free Internet. Breakfast is included in the
price. Accommodation varies from €35 to €80 per night.

Hotel Ibis Faro

E.N. 125 Pontes de Marchil,
Faro 8000-770, Portugal
Tel: 289 893 800
http://www.ibis.com/gb/hotel-1593-ibis-faro/

The Hotel Ibis Faro boasts a bright and modern decor. It is
located near the beach, as well as the enigmatic Ria
Formosa Nature Reserve, which is one of the great natural
attractions of the Algarve. The hotel has a lovely
swimming pool and all rooms have air conditioning,
television, free Wifi Internet and bathroom facilities.

The price includes a large and extensive breakfast buffet selection. The hotel is a participant in the Le Club Accorhotels loyalty program. Accommodation begins at €35.

Places to Eat

Oasis

Marina de Lagos,
Lagos, Portugal

Located on the Lagos Marina, Oasis is English owned and serves a combination of Portuguese and International cuisine. The cafe is open for breakfast, lunch and supper. Try the full English Breakfast or pick from the choice of toasted sandwiches and baguettes, gammon steaks, burgers, pasta and fish and chips. On Friday nights, try the special deal, which allows you to enjoy a meal and drink for only €7.95.

Marco's Bistro

Dunas de Alvor, Loja 16, Alvor,
Portimao, Portugal
Tel: 282 457 548
http://www.marcosalvor.com/

Marco's Bistro provides a friendly setting for enjoying good food at affordable prices. There are various special deals such as the Poolside Special, which comprises the choice of a burger or hot dog plus beverage for €3.50 or the Sunday lunch for €10.95. Some of the dinner highlights include Spicy Chilli Con Carne, homemade lasagne and the Horseshoe Gammon Steak. Lunchtime menu items include sandwiches ranged from €2.00 to €3.95, salads, hot dogs, burgers, French fries and baked potato. There is a breakfast menu as well. Marco's also offers free Wifi access.

Fat Cats Diner

Rodrimar Apartments
Rua Dumfermline,
Albufeira 8200, Portugal
Tel: 966 799 779

The Fat Cats Diner presents a well maintained exterior and boosts atmosphere with regular events such as quizzes and karaoke. The food is well-prepared and great value for money. The menu includes salads, sandwiches, baked potato, with a variety of fillings, fish and chips, gammon steak and English breakfast. Menu items range from €4 for a breakfast to around €10 for the fish and chips.

Restaurante a Taska

Rua do Alportel 38,
Faro
Tel: 289 824 739

For an eatery that is a little off the tourist track, try a local favorite in Faro, namely Restaurante a Taska. On the menu you will find regional specialties such as eel stew and pork with clams. Expect to pay between €13 and €16 for meals and drinks.

Restaurante da Bairrada

Vale Caranguejo,
Tavira 8800-453, Portugal
Tel: 281 324 467

Restaurante da Bairrada is popular with locals and the
expat community of Tavira. Some of the menu highlights
include suckling pig, monkfish kebabs and the popular
steak on a stone, although the restaurant also serves
lighter meals such as omelettes, salads and sandwiches.
Expect to pay between €15 and €20 per person.

Places to Shop

Shopping in Albufeira

There are two main areas you should visit when planning
a shopping excursion in Albufeira. Rua 5 de Outubro is
located near the tunnel that leads to the beach and here
you can expect an interesting mix of clothing shops and
craft traders. In the holiday months, there will also be a
number of temporary stalls. A great place for local crafts
is Infante Dom Henrique House at RuaCândido do Reis
30, which sells hand-woven baskets, ceramics and painted
tiles.

The centrally located Belle Vista Shopping Center is anchored by two supermarkets, but also features a variety of smaller shops and food outlets. The Av. Dr. Francisco SáCarneiro is known as The Strip and the business in this area focuses more on tourist trade. There are several restaurants, bars as well as souvenir shops where you can buy the usual T-shirts and other keepsakes.

A fashion outlet nearby that may be worth exploring is Oceana Boutique on Galarias Nova Oura. Catering in ladies fashion, you would stand a good chance of discovering something here that is both attractive and a little different, sometimes at very reasonable prices. The Algarve Shopping Mall, which is just outside the town, has a selection of over 80 different shops. Over 25 of these cater in fashion and clothing. The mall is off the EN125 highway.

Shopping in Lagos

A street highly recommended for browsing and shopping in Lagos is Rua 25 de Abril, where there is a particularly good selection of outlets offering pottery, ceramics and "azulejos", the distinctive blue tiles used in the mosaics that decorate many a building in the Algarve. Another location, just outside Lagos is Hipercerâmica Paraíso Lda, which sells pottery, leatherwork, cork products and tiles. It can be found on the way to Sagres at EN125, Raposeira which is west of Lagos. Near the marina, you could visit the Lagos Marina Gift Shop, for clothing and keepsakes of this area.

Shopping in Faro

The Forum Algarve on Av. Cáceres Monteiro (http://www.forumalgarve.net/) is a large shopping center near the city Faro, which boasts a beautiful exterior with tiling detail. The complex includes various fashion and home decor shops as well as a supermarket, cinemas and a large food court on the second floor.

One street in Faro with plenty of shopping opportunity is the Rua do Santo Antonio. Do check out Carminho at number 29 and Casa Branca at number 10 for locally crafted items. Other streets worth browsing through are Rua de Francisco Gomes and Rua de Portugal. There is also a market, the Mercado de Faro, that trades every day in the city centre.

Casa das Portas in Tavira

Rua Dr Augusto Silva Carvalho,
Tavira, Portugal
http://www.casadasportas.com/

Located near the Roman bridge, Casa das Portas showcases a beautiful range of original, locally crafted items. Items range from jewellery to ornaments, handbags, ceramics and art prints. The 'Portas' series by Jane Gibbin, which features photographs of doors and windows around Tavira is a prominent theme of the shop.

Gypsy Markets

Nearly every town or city has at least one weekly or monthly market, selling fresh produce, crafts or sometimes antiques. The one in Loulé sells various crafted items such as baskets and ceramics. It trades every second Saturday of the month at Cortelha. Lagos hosts a market on the first Saturday at the municiple stadium, but there is also a fleamarket on the second Saturday at Chinicato.

Tavira's gypsy market is on the third Saturday in Rua Vale Carangueijo. Portimao has a market on the first Monday at Parque de Feiras e Exposições, while Silves has a market near the cemetery on the third Monday of each month.

Printed in Great Britain
by Amazon

25399193R00046